HOW DOES IT WORK?
HELICOPTERS

by Jenny Fretland VanVoorst

pogo

Ideas for Parents and Teachers

Pogo Books let children practice reading informational text while introducing them to nonfiction features such as headings, labels, sidebars, maps, and diagrams, as well as a table of contents, glossary, and index.

Carefully leveled text with a strong photo match offers early fluent readers the support they need to succeed.

Before Reading

• "Walk" through the book and point out the various nonfiction features. Ask the student what purpose each feature serves.

• Look at the glossary together. Read and discuss the words.

Read the Book

• Have the child read the book independently.

• Invite him or her to list questions that arise from reading.

After Reading

• Discuss the child's questions. Talk about how he or she might find answers to those questions.

• Prompt the child to think more. Ask: Have you ever flown in a helicopter before? Does learning how helicopters work make the experience seem more remarkable?

Pogo Books are published by Jump!
5357 Penn Avenue South
Minneapolis, MN 55419
www.jumplibrary.com

Library of Congress Cataloging-in-Publication Data is available at www.loc.gov or upon request from the publisher.

ISBN: 978-1-62031-904-8 (hardcover)
ISBN: 978-1-62031-905-5 (paperback)
ISBN: 978-1-62496-696-5 (ebook)

Editor: Kristine Spanier
Book Designer: Leah Sanders
Photo Researcher: Leah Sanders

Photo Credits: tai11/Shutterstock, cover; roibu/Shutterstock, 1; Ewais/Shutterstock, 3; JackF/iStock, 4 (top); pio3/Shutterstock, 4 (bottom); Photos SS/Shutterstock, 5; Makushin Alexey/Shutterstock, 6-7; Oleg Proskurin/Shutterstock, 8-9; mayo5/iStock, 10-11; alxpin/iStock, 12; Lisa-Blue/iStock, 13; Alphotographic/iStock, 14-15; John Orsbun/Shutterstock, 16; bennymarty/iStock, 17; Art Konovalov/Shutterstock, 18-19; Veja/Shutterstock, 20-21; ChiccoDodiFC/Shutterstock, 20-21 (helicopter); RASimon/iStock, 23.

Printed in the United States of America at Corporate Graphics in North Mankato, Minnesota.

TABLE OF CONTENTS

CHAPTER 1

AMAZING AIRCRAFT

Helicopters are unique flying machines. They can **hover**.

They can fly straight up. They can even fly backward. How can a helicopter do such amazing things? And how does a pilot control it?

It comes down to the **rotor**. That's the huge set of spinning **blades** on top. The rotor creates **lift**. Lift pushes the heavy craft up into the air.

rotor

faster air

lift

slower air

The rotor blades have a shape. It is called an **airfoil**. This shape increases lift. How? It causes air above the blades to move faster than the air below the blades. This changes the **air pressure** around the blades. Less **force** is pushing down on the craft.

The rotor spins. Higher air pressure pushes slower-moving air downward. The moving air creates lift. It pushes the helicopter upward.

CHAPTER 2

LAW OF MOTION IN ACTION

The main rotor blades spin very fast.
How fast? About 500 times a minute!
This motion is necessary for flight.
But it also presents a problem. Why?

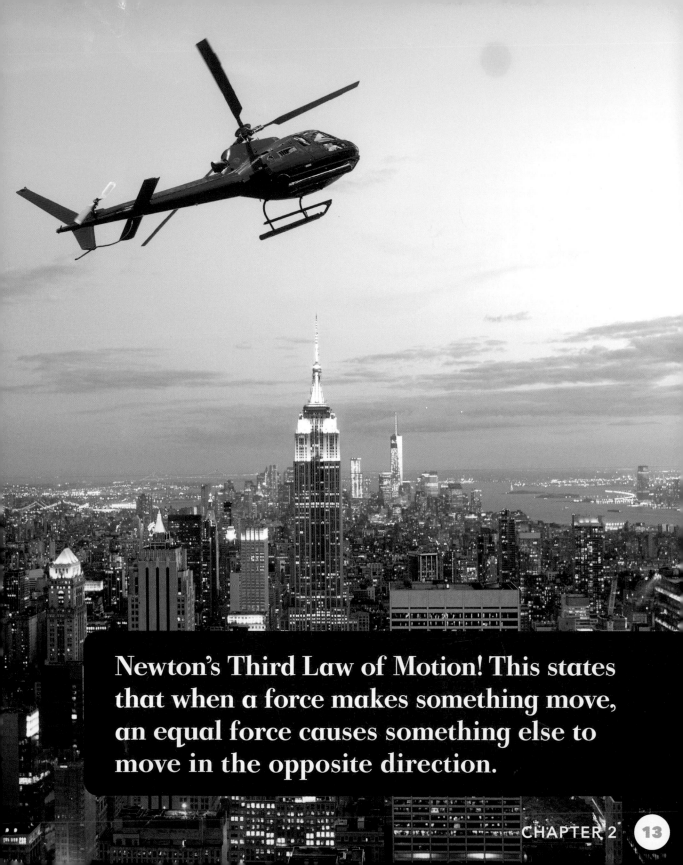

Newton's Third Law of Motion! This states that when a force makes something move, an equal force causes something else to move in the opposite direction.

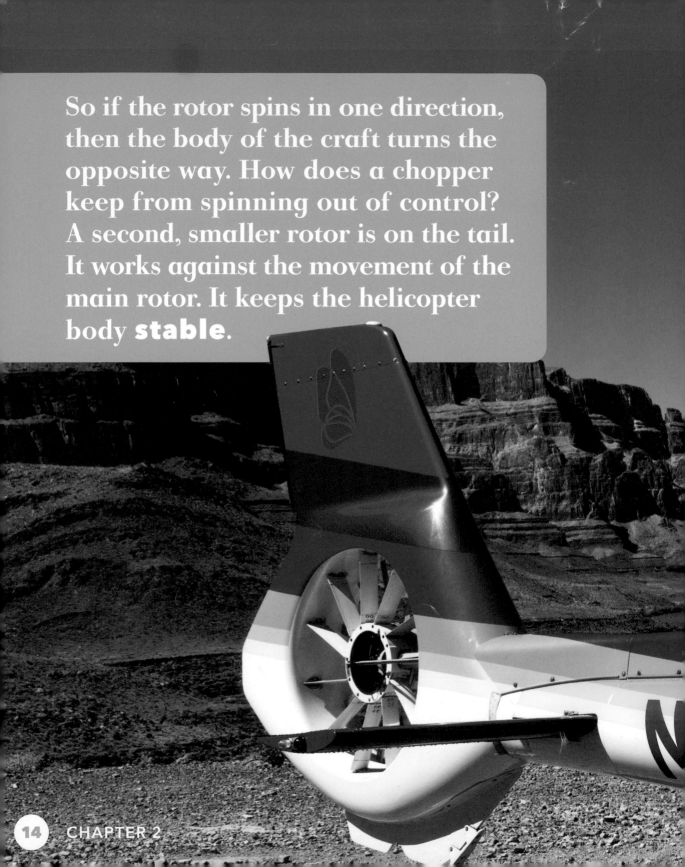

So if the rotor spins in one direction, then the body of the craft turns the opposite way. How does a chopper keep from spinning out of control? A second, smaller rotor is on the tail. It works against the movement of the main rotor. It keeps the helicopter body **stable**.

TAKE A LOOK!

Many parts of a helicopter work together to make it fly. Here are the main parts:

TAIL ROTOR

ROTOR BLADE

COCKPIT

LANDING SKIDS

CHAPTER 3

. . . .

ROTOR BLADES STEER

Keeping a chopper in the air is hard. But **steering** is even more complicated.

This pilot sits in the cockpit. He steers the chopper. How? By changing the angle of the rotor blades. This changes the lift direction. How does that work?

To turn, pilots need to make more lift on one side. They angle the blades back and forth as they spin. This tilts the chopper and steers it.

Helicopters can fly many ways. Pilots have a lot to control, including laws of **physics**. Look up in the sky. The next time you see a chopper, you'll know how it flies!

ACTIVITIES & TOOLS

BE A CHOPPER

You can imitate the movement of a helicopter with your own body! Spin around with your arms outstretched. Your arms are like a helicopter's rotor blades and your body is the mast. Your shoulder joints work like the hinges on the rotor blades, so you can steer by changing the angle at which your arms meet the air. Just swivel your arms at the shoulders as you're turning. Do you feel yourself tilting as you spin? You're steering! Have fun imitating a helicopter, and be careful not to crash!

airfoil: A surface designed to produce a specific reaction from the air through which it moves.

air pressure: The force exerted onto a surface by the weight of the air.

blades: Arms of a propeller or a similar machine.

exhaust: The gas that escapes from an engine.

force: An influence, such as a push or pull, that produces a change in the speed or direction of an object's motion.

hover: To float over a place or object.

lift: An upward force that overcomes the weight of an aircraft to keep it in the sky.

physics: The science that deals with matter and energy and their actions upon each other in the fields of mechanics, heat, light, electricity, sound, and the atomic nucleus.

rotor: The set of rotating blades that supports a helicopter in flight.

stable: Not easily moved or changed.

steering: Directing the path that something follows.

turboshaft engines: Gas turbine engines that power devices through a transmission system.

INDEX

TO LEARN MORE

Learning more is as easy as 1, 2, 3.

1) Go to www.factsurfer.com

2) Enter "helicopters" into the search box.

3) Click the "Surf" button to see a list of websites.

With factsurfer, finding more information is just a click away.